THE WHALE WHO WON HEARTS!

And More True Stories of Adventures With Animals

By Brian Skerry
With Kathleen Weidner Zoehfeld

NATIONAL
GEOGRAPHIC

WASHINGTON, D.C.

Published by the National Geographic Society

John M. Fahey, *Chairman of the Board and Chief Executive Officer*
Declan Moore, *Executive Vice President; President, Publishing and Travel*
Melina Gerosa Bellows, *Publisher and Chief Creative Officer, Books, Kids, and Family*

Prepared by the Book Division
Hector Sierra, *Senior Vice President and General Manager*
Nancy Laties Feresten, *Senior Vice President, Kids Publishing and Media*
Jennifer Emmett, *Vice President, Editorial Director, Kids Books*
Eva Absher-Schantz, *Design Director, Kids Publishing and Media*
Jay Sumner, *Director of Photography, Kids Publishing*
R. Gary Colbert, *Production Director*
Jennifer A. Thornton, *Director of Managing Editorial*

Staff for This Book
Becky Baines, Shelby Alinsky, *Project Editors*
Marfé Ferguson Delano, *Editor*
Kelley Miller, *Senior Photo Editor*
Amanda Larsen, *Art Director*
Ruth Ann Thompson, *Designer*
Ariane Szu-Tu, *Editorial Assistant*
Callie Broaddus, *Design Production Assistant*
Margaret Leist, *Illustrations Assistant*
Grace Hill, *Associate Managing Editor*
Joan Gossett, *Production Editor*
Lewis R. Bassford, *Production Manager*
Susan Borke, *Legal and Business Affairs*

Production Services
Phillip L. Schlosser,
    Senior Vice President
Chris Brown, *Vice President,
    NG Book Manufacturing*
George Bounelis,
    Senior Production Manager
Nicole Elliott, *Director of Production*
Rachel Faulise, *Manager*
Robert L. Barr, *Manager*

The National Geographic Society is one of the world's largest nonprofit scientific and educational organizations. Founded in 1888 to "increase and diffuse geographic knowledge," the Society's mission is to inspire people to care about the planet. It reaches more than 400 million people worldwide each month through its official journal, *National Geographic*, and other magazines; National Geographic Channel; television documentaries; music; radio; films; books; DVDs; maps; exhibitions; live events; school publishing programs; interactive media; and merchandise. National Geographic has funded more than 10,000 scientific research, conservation, and exploration projects and supports an education program promoting geographic literacy.

For more information, please visit www.nationalgeographic.com, call 1-800-NGS LINE (647-5463), or write to the following address:

National Geographic Society, 1145 17th Street N.W., Washington, D.C. 20036-4688 U.S.A.

Visit us online at www.nationalgeographic.com/books

For librarians and teachers: www.ngchildrensbooks.org

National Geographic supports K–12 educators with ELA Common Core Resources. Visit natgeoed.org/commoncore for more information.

More for kids from National Geographic: kids.nationalgeographic.com

For information about special discounts for bulk purchases, please contact National Geographic Books Special Sales: ngspecsales@ngs.org

For rights or permissions inquiries, please contact National Geographic Books Subsidiary Rights: ngbookrights@ngs.org

Trade paperback ISBN:
    978-1-4263-1520-6
Reinforced library edition ISBN:
    978-1-4263-1521-3

Printed in China
14/RRDS/1

Table of CONTENTS

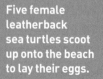

Five female leatherback sea turtles scoot up onto the beach to lay their eggs.

Quest for LIVING DINOSAURS

This is me, photographer Brian Skerry, with my special underwater camera and lights. I'm getting ready to dive.

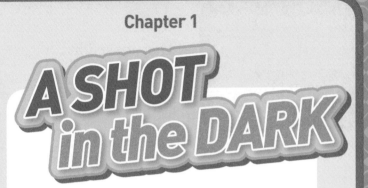

Chapter 1

A SHOT in the DARK

It was a warm night in May. I was walking along a beach in Trinidad (sounds like TRIH-nuh-dad), an island in the Caribbean (sounds like CARE-uh-BEE-un) Sea. It was almost midnight. The ocean waves rumbled and crashed onto the sand. Behind the beach, palm trees swayed in the damp breeze.

Suddenly, a few yards down, I spotted dark shapes on the sand.

They looked like huge rocks. But they were leatherback sea turtles! They were here to do something sea turtles have been doing for more than 100 million years. And I was hoping to shoot them. With my camera, that is!

My name is Brian Skerry. I'm an underwater wildlife photographer. It's my job to take pictures of animals that live in the sea.

I fell in love with the sea when I was a child. I grew up in a small town in Massachusetts. We lived about an hour's drive from the ocean. I was always asking my parents to take me there.

When I wasn't at the beach, I was

reading books or watching TV shows about ocean life. I really admired the sea turtles. It was fun to imagine gliding with them through miles of deep, blue water.

When I was 15, I tried scuba diving. It was in my family's swimming pool. I was sitting in the shallow end. I had the scuba tank on my back. Hoses attached to the tank would bring air to my mouthpiece. I'll never forget putting that mouthpiece in and taking my first breath underwater. All I could think was, "Wow! I have discovered a whole new world!"

As I grew up, I practiced diving. I studied photography in college. I began taking underwater photos. Finally, I landed my dream job. I was hired to take photos for *National Geographic* magazine.

And that's what brought me to Trinidad. I was there to photograph sea turtles for National Geographic.

Sea turtles are reptiles. Like all reptiles, they breathe air. But unlike most reptiles, sea turtles don't live on land. They spend nearly their entire lives in the ocean. That's why they're called marine reptiles.

One hundred million years ago, dinosaurs ruled the land. At that time, many types of marine reptiles lived in the oceans. Giant, long-necked plesiosaurs (sounds like PLEEZ-ee-oh-soars) and sharp-toothed ichthyosaurs (sounds like ICK-thee-oh-soars) swam the seas. Earth's first sea turtles swam with them.

Dinosaurs died out 65 million years ago. Marine reptiles went extinct then, too—all of them except for sea turtles, that is.

Seven types of sea turtles are still around today. The leatherback is the largest of them all. Leatherbacks can grow to more than seven feet (2 m) long. They can weigh more than 2,000 pounds (900 kg).

Other types of sea turtles have hard shells. Not leatherback sea turtles. They have thick, leathery skin. It's what gives them their name.

My assistant Mauricio (sounds like moh-REE-cee-oh) Handler was with me on the beach. As we watched, the giant female leatherbacks began to dig their nests and lay their eggs. Female leatherbacks always lay their eggs on warm, sandy beaches. Usually they return to the same beach where they were born.

Turtles in Trouble

Sadly, leatherback turtles are in danger of extinction. People have been hunting leatherbacks for centuries. But over the past 30 years, too many have been killed for their meat. People raided nests and took all the eggs. Today, new laws help protect nesting leatherbacks and their eggs. But they still face many dangers. They get tangled in fishnets. They get hooked on longlines meant to catch large fish. Houses and hotels have also been built on some of the leatherbacks' favorite nesting beaches.

I moved in close to one of the turtles. Leatherbacks only come out when it is dark. I knew the camera flashbulb would disturb her. So I would rely on the moonlight.

The turtle found a spot she liked. She made a shallow pit in the sand with her front flippers. Once she was comfy, she dug a deep hole with her hind flippers. She took long, deep breaths as she dug. To me, it was like a sound from the prehistoric (sounds like pre-hih-STORE-ick) past! She laid more than 80 round, white eggs in the hole. Then she covered them with sand.

We watched as the turtle headed back to the water. Having a chance to photograph this huge creature in the wild was thrilling—almost like seeing a living dinosaur!

A newly hatched baby leatherback scurries to the sea. It will spend the rest of its life in the water.

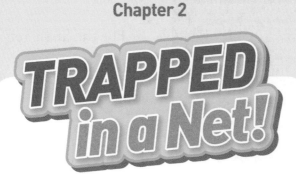

Chapter 2

TRAPPED in a Net!

It takes 60 to 70 days for a leatherback's babies to come out of their eggs. While we were taking photos of the nesting leatherbacks, eggs from other nests began to hatch. We stopped to take photos as the tiny, striped hatchlings hurried across the sand. Their mothers were long gone. Leatherback babies must look to the sea for food and protection.

Leatherbacks can dive as deep as 4,000 feet (1,219 m). Even the most skilled human scuba divers cannot dive much deeper than 1,000 feet (305 m).

For the lucky few who make it to adulthood, there aren't many ocean creatures that can harm them. But humans have created new problems for these ancient (sounds like ANE-chunt) animals. I wanted to see for myself the dangers leatherbacks face once they leave the shore. It was time to get into the water!

I talked to local fishermen and found one who was interested in helping. He said leatherbacks sometimes got tangled in his fishnets. He did what he could to save them. But sometimes he was too late. If a tangled turtle is not pulled to the surface soon enough, it will drown.

The fisherman said we could follow him while he fished. If any turtles got caught, we could see how it happened. Maybe we could even help. We rented a small boat. The captain of our boat helped us sail close behind the fishing boat.

We watched as the fisherman set out a mile (1.6 km) of fishnet. Floats held up the top edge of the net. The rest of it hung down in the water, like a curtain. After several hours, the fisherman pulled in his net. Dozens of fish were caught in it. He put the fish in his boat. Then he set the net out again.

Our captain moved our boat slowly alongside the net. I sat in the front of the boat. The stars shone brightly above us. I kept an eye on the net below. I had my

fins, mask, and air tank ready, in case
I needed to dive.

Later that night, Mauricio and I
spotted an adult turtle in the net. I quickly
pulled on my diving gear and went over
the side. As I swam down, I could see the
leatherback struggling.

Leatherbacks never stop swimming.
The turtle paddled and paddled with its
long flippers. The more it paddled, the more
tangled it became. I took a few pictures of
it. Then I had to help it. I grabbed my
knife and began to cut the net.

As I worked, the current began to wrap
me up in the net, too. I had to stop helping
the turtle and cut myself free first. Then I
cut the turtle loose. I watched as it swam
off gracefully, into the darkness of the sea.

Chowing Down

Jellyfish, or jellies, are a leatherback's favorite food. Jellies are mostly water, with a few minerals and a dash of protein thrown in. How do leatherbacks grow so big on a jelly diet? The answer: they eat a LOT of jellies. Scientists videotaped one leatherback eating 69 jellies in three hours. Each jelly weighed about ten pounds (4.5 kg). That's 690 pounds (313 kg) of jellies! A leatherback's throat is lined with three-inch (7.6-cm) spines. These spines help the turtle swallow its very slippery prey—and keep the prey from coming back up.

I found this leatherback swimming in deep water. The two yellow fish clinging to her side are called remoras.

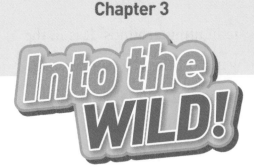

Now I had pictures of a leatherback underwater. But I wanted to take photos of one swimming. I knew I'd find turtles swimming around Trinidad. But the water there is too murky to get good photos. I needed to find leatherbacks in clear water. So I went to the other side of the world. To the Pacific Ocean!

I headed for one of the turtles'

favorite hunting grounds. It is in the deep water off the Kai (sounds like KEY) Islands in Indonesia (sounds like in-doh-NEE-zhuh).

My assistant Jeff Wildermuth joined me on this trip. When we got to the Kai Islands, we talked to some local fishermen. They gave us tips on how to find turtles.

The fishermen go out to sea in long, narrow boats. Boats like this have been used in these islands for thousands of years. I decided to use one of them to search for leatherbacks. I knew it could be dangerous. The boats are very tippy when the waves get steep! But this was my best bet for getting close to the turtles.

The local people told us they often found turtles around a certain island.

Jeff and I set up our tents on the beach there. Then we decided to try our luck.

Jeff and I eased our boat off the sand and into the choppy water. We watched for the glint of a black turtle moving under the silvery waves. Meanwhile, the sun blazed down on us. We gulped water from our water bottles. We paddled around the whole island, searching. Before we knew it, the sun was going down. We hadn't seen one turtle.

Back at camp, we checked to make sure there were no scorpions under our sleeping bags. We pulled our mosquito nets around us. Then we fell fast asleep.

The next morning, we went off in our boat again. Hour after hour, we watched and waited for leatherbacks. No luck.

What You Can Do

Here are some ways you can help sea turtles continue to survive:

• Make less trash, and pick up trash at the beach. Plastic bags can end up being washed into the sea. Many leatherbacks are killed when they eat plastic bags. To them, the bags look like jellyfish.

• Stay away from sea turtle nesting areas. If you live near a nesting beach, keep your lights low during nesting season.

• Design a poster. Write a report. Give a talk. Help people understand how important Earth's oceans are!

Scientists have learned that it takes 20 to 30 years for a female leatherback to grow old enough to lay eggs. But over the last 30 years, people have been stealing the eggs from leatherback nests. It's clear that this has hurt the turtles. It has left very few young ones to grow up in the sea.

Day after day, Jeff and I waited and watched. We felt sad that this vast ocean is now nearly empty of leatherbacks.

On the fourth day, we spotted our first turtle! I grabbed my camera and slipped quickly into the water. I didn't put on any of my diving gear, except for my fins. Leatherbacks are fast swimmers, and I thought the gear would slow me down. Still, I couldn't keep up. The leatherback was gone in a flash.

In three weeks, we saw leatherbacks only three times. I tried to take some good photos. But I had no luck.

Finally, near the end of our stay, we spotted a beautiful female. She was coming up for a breath. And she was moving pretty slowly. I slipped into the water and swam alongside her. She saw me and began to dive.

She made slow, steady strokes with her flippers. She moved through the water easily, like a bird flying through the air. I swam as hard as I could to keep up. Fishy tagalongs called remoras (sounds like reh-MORE-ahs) clung to her sides. A school of little fish swam out in front of her.

Nearly out of breath, I managed to get a few shots. I hoped they would be good ones! Exhausted, I stopped kicking. Then I drifted to the surface. Jeff and I watched as the turtle faded into the blue.

That night, I checked my shots. We had searched the sea for weeks. Some days, we didn't think we'd survive the brutal sun and biting bugs. But yes! We had finally gotten a good photo of a leatherback in the wild. It's the one on page 20 of this book.

> **Did You Know?**
>
> **Leatherbacks** swim longer distances than any other turtle. They've been tracked traveling more than 6,500 miles (10,460 km).

The giant turtle looked like a living starship traveling through her underwater universe. We could only hope that our work would help people understand what these awesome animals are going through.

Surrounded by sea ice, a mother harp seal and I take a look at each other.

The Ice,
the Seals,
AND ME

A white harp seal pup is safe on the ice. The pup's mom looks on from the water.

Chapter 1

The Whitecoats ARRIVE

Harp seals live in the icy waters of the North Atlantic and Arctic Oceans. But every year in early spring, thousands of them swim south to Canada's Gulf of St. Lawrence. The females gather in small groups on top of the sea ice. That's where they give birth to their pups.

Most photographers use helicopters to reach the seals.

Harp seals get
their name from the
harp-shaped band of
dark fur found on the
backs of adults.

That way they can
stay on the ice for a
few hours and then
fly home. I wanted
more than a few hours with the seals.
I wanted to take photos of them at all
different times of day.

In early spring I flew to the Magdalen
(sounds like MAG-duh-lin) Islands, a
group of small islands in the gulf. Fishing is
a way of life for the people here. At this
time of year, the sea ice begins to break up.
The fishermen get ready to sail. They will
stay out in the gulf for many days at a time.
That's exactly what I wanted to do!

Some local fishermen agreed to take me
out with them. The captain and his two-
man crew welcomed me and my assistant

Sean (sounds like SHAWN) Whelan aboard. Their 65-foot (20-m) boat would be our home for the next 17 days.

I stared out at the frozen sea. I couldn't imagine how we were going to get anywhere. Thick sheets of ice still covered the water. There were just a few cracks here and there. The captain told me not to worry. He knew how to move the boat through the narrow openings. Plus, this was no ordinary fishing boat! It was built tough. The body, or hull, of the boat was made of thick steel.

Not long after we left the dock, our ship's strength was tested. We found ourselves iced in. We were completely surrounded by ice. But the captain knew how to break out. He powered the boat up on top of the ice. We could hear the steel hull crunching the ice below. Once we'd made a new crack, we sailed on a little farther. Then we hit solid ice again. And again the captain powered the ship through.

After several hours of this, we spotted a group of harp seals on the ice up ahead. I watched them for a while, from the deck. It looked like they would soon give birth to their pups. I couldn't wait to get out on the ice with them!

We stayed near the seals for many days. Each morning I woke up at six and put on my thermal underwear, socks, fleece sweater, ski goggles, parka, and warm boots. I grabbed my cameras. Then I walked quietly out onto the ice.

Sleek Swimmers

Harp seals are swift hunters. They dive as deep as 1,000 feet (305 meters) in search of fish, shrimp, and crabs to eat. They can stay underwater for as long as 15 minutes. But like all mammals, they must come up to the surface to breathe. There are three different groups of harp seals in the Arctic. In the spring, each group returns to its favorite breeding area, either in the Gulf of St. Lawrence, the Greenland Sea, or the White Sea. Adult harp seals grow to be five to six feet (1.5 to 1.8 m) long. They can weigh up to 400 pounds (180 kg).

On my very first day, a few pups were born. Newborn harp seals are light yellow. In just a day or two, they turn snowy white. The young pups are called "whitecoats." Their fluffy fur protects them from the freezing air. But it doesn't keep them warm in the icy cold water. If they fall in, they will quickly get too cold and drown.

Each pup stayed close to the spot where it was born. Like most babies, they spent a lot of time sleeping. On sunny days, the ice melted under them, creating seal-shaped cradles in the ice.

After giving birth, the mother seals spent much of their time in the water. But they were never far from their babies. When a pup was hungry it cried, *Mmaaaa! Mmaaaa!* Then up popped its mother through a crack in the ice. She sniffed the pup, just to be sure it was hers. Then she flopped on her side and let the pup nurse.

I was amazed at how quickly the pups grew. Seal milk has ten times the fat of cow's milk. Pups gain five pounds (2.3 kg) a day on their moms' milk. By the time they're ten days old, they weigh more than 70 pounds (32 kg). Mother harp seals only nurse their pups for 12 days. Then they swim off for good, leaving the pups on their own. These pups have to grow fast!

By midmorning each day, I headed back to the ship. I ate a hearty breakfast of eggs, bacon, and sausages, and plenty of hot coffee. Then it was time to dive.

Here I am, under the sea ice with my camera and lights. A special diving suit helps protect me from the supercold seawater.

Chapter 2

Cold water can be deadly if a diver's not prepared. And here the seawater is supercold! It's even colder than the temperature at which ice cubes freeze solid. In sub-freezing temperatures like this, an unprotected human can only survive a few moments.

First, I pulled on layers of thermal underwear. Then I put

on my dry suit. Unlike a wet suit, which divers use in warm water, a dry suit keeps water out. Mine has boots and gloves attached. Next, I pulled on two separate hoods. The first one, called an "ice hood," covers my head and face. It has holes for my eyes and mouth. The second hood is open for my face, but it protects my head and neck.

Last, I put on my mask and settled my air tank on my back. Then I slipped through a hole in the ice. The ice above my head looked like an upside-down mountain range. Icy peaks and valleys rolled on as far as I could see. Sunbeams sparkled through gaps in the ice. It was a crystal kingdom of emerald green that glowed from above.

The mother seals glided gracefully through the water. They were shy about getting too close to me. So I hid behind a ledge of ice, just below one of their breathing holes. I waited for good shots to come along. And I waited. Often, the main skill a wildlife photographer needs is patience.

While they were nursing their pups, the moms hardly had any chance to eat. After 12 days, they were getting very hungry! One by one, they began to swim away. They headed north to feed.

The pups now had a thick layer of fat, called blubber, under their skin. At the same time, they were beginning to shed their white fur.

Did You Know?

Adult harp seals can swim more than 2,500 miles (4,023 km) from their hunting grounds to their breeding grounds.

Underneath was a smooth, speckled gray coat. This new fur, along with their fat, would help keep them warm in the icy water.

Left all alone on the ice, the spotted gray pups cried for their moms. But no moms returned. The pups began to slide into the icy sea for a few minutes at a time. Then they crawled back up onto the ice. At this stage, they're called "beaters," because of the awkward way they beat the water with their flippers.

The pups were easier to photograph underwater than the adults. They were still beginning swimmers. But each day they swam a little longer and dove a little deeper. They were figuring out the watery world that would soon be their home.

One evening, as twilight settled in,

I took a few more photos on the ice. Then I climbed aboard the boat for the night. I listened to the pups, still calling for their moms in the darkness. I felt good about our work so far. But trouble can arrive quickly on the ice.

At two o'clock in the morning, one of the fishermen shook me awake. "The captain wants to see you," he said. I climbed the ladder to the ship's control room. I found the captain staring out at a swirling world of white. There was a blizzard raging outside.

"The ice is against the hull now," he said. "We'll be crushed sometime soon and will sink."

This was a tough boat. But now hurricane-force winds were slamming giant slabs of sea ice against us. Few boats can withstand that. The captain radioed for help. But we were far from the islands. It could take a long time for help to arrive.

The captain ordered us to get into our survival suits. In warm places, a good life jacket may be enough to help you survive a shipwreck. Near the Arctic, you need a thick, head-to-toe suit that will help you float and keep you warm.

For two hours, Sean and I sat on deck with the crew. We listened to the wind howl. We waited for the groaning sound of buckling, or crumpling, steel. In the glow of the ship's spotlight, we stared at the huge slabs of ice surrounding us. The idea that we might have to jump off the boat and onto that ice was truly terrifying.

Harp Seal Talk

Harp seals have good hearing, especially underwater. When a mother seal is underwater, she can hear her pup when it cries for her up on the ice. When pups play together on the ice, they make cute mumbling sounds. Adults call to each other, too. Big male seals growl and warble at each other. This can mean "back off!" Adults are really chatty when they're looking for mates. Scientists have counted more than 19 different sounds harp seals make underwater. These include chirps, trills, and clicks.

This whitecoat looked right at me with its big, dark eyes. The pup's fluffy fur protects it from freezing air.

SINK or SWIM!

Lucky for us, the steel did not buckle. And sometime after four o'clock, we were rescued! A huge Canadian Coast Guard ship arrived. It cut a path through the ice. We followed it. Nine hours later, we made it back to the Magdalen Islands.

For us, the blizzard was a brush with disaster. But it was just an extra-exciting night on the ice for the harp seals. They are at home here.

I knew the pups I had photographed would soon be swimming north. As long as they're on the ice, seals are easy targets for hungry polar bears. Still, it's safer for them in the gulf than it is up north. That's why the moms come here to give birth. Fewer polar bears stalk the ice here.

Once the pups are ready to swim north, they will stay in the water most of their lives. Then, sharks and orcas, or killer whales, will become a big danger. It's safer for pups to practice swimming in the gulf. They can become fast swimmers before having to face their natural enemies.

Did You Know?

A mother harp seal can pick out her baby from hundreds of others by its smell.

In the gulf, humans are the pups' biggest threat. They have long hunted harp seals for their oil, fur, and skin. In the 1940s, the white coats of the newborn pups became popular. Hundreds of thousands of pups were killed to make fur coats.

In 1987, it became against the law to hunt and kill the "whitecoat" pups. But by then, harp seals were in danger of extinction. Today, humans still hunt harp seals. But there are limits on how many seals hunters can take.

Harp seals are slowly making a comeback. But the danger is far from over. In recent years, thick sea ice has begun to melt. It is starting to vanish from the gulf. If that ice goes, the seals may no longer have any safe places to give birth.

Vanishing Ice

All over the globe, the climate is changing. As people burn fossil fuels, such as oil and coal, carbon dioxide (sounds like die-OX-ide) is released into the atmosphere (sounds like AT-muhs-fear). Carbon dioxide is a greenhouse gas. It causes Earth's atmosphere to trap the sun's warmth, much the way the glass in a greenhouse does. As the amount of carbon dioxide increases, more and more of the sun's heat is trapped. This is causing Earth's average temperature to rise. And as the Earth gets warmer, more sea ice melts.

During my time in the gulf, I saw many pups die because they fell into the water before they were ready. In the future, harp seals may have to have their pups farther north. The ice may be more solid up there. But there are also more killer whales and polar bears.

The more I saw of harp seals, the more I admired them. Even after our scary night on the boat, I looked forward to getting out on the ice with them again. This time I went out in a helicopter! My hands and feet ached and went numb with the cold. I had to wear ski goggles to shield my eyes from the biting wind and snow. But the thrill of seeing these creatures in their beautiful frozen world made it all worth it!

While my buddy Jim Johnson was taking a picture of his friend Wilma, a beluga whale, I took this photo of him.

THE WHALE
Who Won
HEARTS

People in a canoe come out to meet Wilma as she swims with a diver.

A NEW Friend!

When I was a kid, I loved learning about whales. I sometimes even dreamed about having a whale as my best friend. I'd put on my mask, snorkel, and fins. Then I'd swim back and forth in my backyard swimming pool. All the time I'd be imagining that I was deep under the ocean waves, with a whale as my guide. What a magical experience it would be, to explore the ocean with a whale as a friend!

Of course, whales are wild animals. They hunt and swim together in small groups called pods. They don't usually make friends with humans.

Now that I'm an underwater photographer, I sometimes get asked to take photos of whales. To get those photos, I go out into the ocean and search for the whales. I never thought a whale might come find me! But that's just what happened to an old diving buddy of mine.

His name is Jim Johnson. Jim lives in Nova Scotia (sounds like NO-vah SKO-shah), in Canada. One day, Jim called me and said that the most amazing thing had happened. A young female beluga whale had come into the bay near his home. And, he said, he had become good friends with her. I could hardly believe it! Jim told me to come on up and meet her.

When I got there, Jim told me the whole story. A few months earlier, some local fishermen had spotted a beluga whale in Chedabucto (sounds like shed-ah-BOUK-toe) Bay. Belugas normally live in the ice-cold waters of the Arctic Ocean. The fishermen knew it was unusual to see a beluga as far south as Nova Scotia. They figured she was just passing through. But a few days later, they saw her again. They told their families and friends about the lonely white whale in the bay.

Chedabucto Bay is a peaceful place. Green, wooded hills line its shores.

Eagles soar in the sky above. Fishing boats rock gently in the quiet harbor. No one knew why the beluga stopped there. Maybe it felt like a welcoming place. Before long, people all around the bay began talking about her. *Why was she still here?* they wondered. She looked young. Maybe she was lost and alone.

The young whale seemed to like the red buoy (sounds like BOO-ee) that bobbed in the middle of the bay. Buoys are floating signs that are anchored in place. They help fishermen and other boaters find their way. Very often, when fishermen passed this buoy, they would see the whale. The buoy's rusty anchor chain rattled and clinked as it rocked in the waves. The buoy's small bell clanged.

Beluga whales are often called white whales. They are among the world's smallest whales. Adults can measure up to 20 feet (6 m) long. Males can weigh up to 3,000 pounds (1,360 kg). Belugas hunt for fish, squid, and shrimp. They also eat crabs and marine worms. Beluga whales can dive as deep as 3,300 feet (1,000 m). They can stay underwater for as long as 25 minutes. But they must come up to the surface to breathe. Like most whales, a beluga breathes air through a blowhole on top of its head.

Whales sing and call to one another across great distances underwater. Beluga whales are very chatty. They are constantly making all kinds of sounds. They chirp and squeak. They clang and whistle. Maybe the young whale felt comforted by the buoy's constant clinking and clanging.

It didn't take long for Jim to hear about the white whale. He's lived on the shore of Chedabucto Bay all his life. He has traveled around the world in great sailing ships. He has lived among seals in the frozen north. He has searched for treasure off the sandy shores of tropical islands. He has been face to face with all kinds of ocean life. But, just like me, one thing he had always dreamed of was swimming with a whale. Jim was thrilled to learn a young beluga was right in his own "backyard." He couldn't wait to meet her.

Jim got his diving gear ready. He loaded it onto his small, inflatable boat. Then he motored his little boat across the water to a small, rocky beach. From here he could see the red buoy. He pulled his boat up on the beach. He put

Did You Know?

Newborn belugas are dark gray. Over the next five years, they grow lighter and lighter in color.

on his diving gear and slipped into the water. He swam down about 20 feet (6 m). He wasn't sure what to expect. He hoped to see the white whale. But he didn't think she'd come very close to him.

Wilma loved to have her picture taken! Here she is by the red buoy.

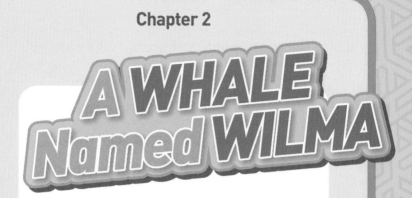

Chapter 2

A WHALE Named WILMA

Jim stared out into the green water. He could see some seashells on the bottom. A few small fish swam past. For what seemed like ages, that is all he saw. He knelt on the bottom. He shivered. He didn't think he could stay under much longer. Then, from out of nowhere, the whale appeared!

She swam slowly toward him at first. Then she moved away,

disappearing into the murky water like a ghost. But she soon came back. She circled around him. And then she stopped right in front of him. Jim stayed very still. His heart pounded. This was no ghost! Right before his eyes, just inches away, was a wild beluga whale.

Very slowly, Jim stretched out his hand. The whale stared at him. Jim wanted to pet her, but he didn't want to frighten her. He waited. She moved toward him. Then, very gently, she pushed the top of her head against his palm. Jim rubbed her head. He ran his hand down her side. She let him stroke her back. Then, as quickly as she had appeared, she swam away into the sea.

A wild whale! He had reached out and petted a wild whale!

As the weeks went by, people continued to spot the young beluga in the bay. They began to think of her as a member of their community. Someone began calling her Wilma, and the name stuck.

Every day, Jim put on his diving gear and swam out to meet Wilma. Much to his surprise, Wilma seemed to like his company. Their friendship grew quickly. But it was not always easy to find Wilma in the murky water. Jim had to think of a way to let her know when he was there.

He knew that whales in the wild call to each other to stay in touch. They also make clicking sounds that help them find their way. When the clicks hit an object such as a fish or rock, the sounds bounce back as echoes. By listening to the echoes, belugas can figure out where and what something is. This is called echolocation (sounds like EH-ko-lo-KAY-shun).

Jim wondered if he could create a call that would get Wilma's attention. Then, using echolocation, maybe she could find him in the water. He got an idea. He picked up two stones and banged them together underwater. It worked like a charm! A few minutes later, up swam Wilma. She knew exactly where he was. From then on, Jim used this signal to let Wilma know he had come to visit. Within ten minutes, he would spot the whale swimming his way.

Melon Head

The beluga's forehead is very unusual. It is big and rounded. It feels like a balloon filled with warm butter. That "balloon" is called the melon. It is actually a fatty lens. The lenses in a pair of eyeglasses focus light. The beluga's melon focuses sound. It focuses the clicks belugas make when they are echolocating. A beluga can change the shape of its melon whenever it needs to. This lets it point its clicks in different directions and focus the clicks at different distances.

Wilma swims below a boy floating with a life jacket. The beluga even rubs her back against his foot.

A DREAM COME TRUE

I was blown away by Jim's story! I couldn't wait to get some photos of him with his new friend.

The next morning after breakfast, Jim took me to meet Wilma. We got into our diving gear and slipped into the water. Jim banged two rocks together, and Wilma soon appeared. It thrilled me to meet her! Together, she and I searched the seafloor for treasures.

We found sand dollars and clam shells. Wilma seemed curious about everything.

Every now and then, she would turn upside down and rub her head on the bottom. That's a good way to scratch your head, when you don't have hands!

Taking photos of Wilma was so much fun. She loved to ham it up for the camera. Later in the morning, she started a game of catch with a piece of kelp, a type of seaweed. She plucked a frond of kelp from the bottom. Then she swam up to the surface with it and let it go. As the kelp drifted down, Wilma dove under it and caught it on her head. Then she swam back up and started the game all over again.

Jim and I laughed at her silly game. He told me that once he accidentally dropped his car keys over the side of the boat. He groaned as he watched them sink into the water. Without much hope, he put on his diving gear and got ready to go looking for them. But before he even got into the water, Wilma popped up with the keys in her mouth. What a great friend!

After a long morning of playing and exploring, Wilma took a rest near the red buoy. Jim floated quietly nearby, and Wilma moved in close. She looked like a big puppy getting ready to snuggle up on the couch. She loved having the top of her head scratched. As Jim petted her, her eyes closed. She seemed to go into a trance.

A Whale of a Challenge

When the Arctic Ocean freezes in winter, beluga whales swim south to warmer waters. If they wait too long to leave, they can get trapped by the Arctic ice. Then they will be easy targets for hungry polar bears and orcas. But human hunters are the belugas' biggest threat. Over the years, overfishing has nearly wiped out some populations. Today, laws limit the fishing of belugas. In some areas, however, beluga whales are still in danger of going extinct.

When we climbed back into the boat to head home, Wilma rubbed along the boat's smooth sides. Jim reached down to say goodbye, and the beluga took his hand gently into her mouth.

Jim told me that he sometimes saw Wilma playing with pilot whales. Sometimes she swam with seals, or with the local divers who gathered sea urchins. People came in boats, canoes, and kayaks to meet her. Of all her visitors, Wilma seemed to love children the most. She let them touch her head and stroke her sides. But Wilma never had the company of her own kind. Jim knew that Wilma was lonely.

Exploring the sea with Wilma was my dream come true. I wanted to stay with her forever. But I had to go home. I was sad to leave Wilma. But I was happy that she had Jim as a friend.

Wilma lived in the bay for many more years. Then one day, I got a call from Jim. Earlier that spring, he had put on his diving gear and gone out to look for Wilma as usual. He peered through the water, but he couldn't find her. He picked up two stones and banged them together. This time, his signal did not work.

Jim got back into his boat. He sailed all around the bay. He returned the next day, and the day after that. Wilma was nowhere to be found. Over the next few months, Jim checked the bay from time to time. But in his heart, he knew that Wilma was gone.

I knew how sad Jim felt. We talked about his special friendship with Wilma. Although he would always miss her, maybe this was for the best. She was a wild animal, free to roam the sea. She needed to find other beluga whales. Maybe she would even start a family. Wilma had come into the bay on her own. She had left on her own. And that's the way it should be.

Jim and I like to imagine that Wilma is out there in the wide sea, having adventures with other whales. We wonder if she's telling them the story of her life among humans. We hope one day we'll see her again. As long as we live, none of us who met Wilma will ever forget this magical gift from the sea.

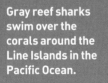

Gray reef sharks swim over the corals around the Line Islands in the Pacific Ocean.

THE REEF Where SHARKS RULE

I took this photo of a diver feeding a shark a fish. He used special gloves to protect his hands from accidental bites.

Chapter 1

HOOKED ON SHARKS

'll never forget the first time I swam with a shark. It was almost 30 years ago. At that time, most people thought of sharks as sharp-toothed killing machines. The last thing any diver wanted was to run into a shark! But I had a chance to help a group of scientists. They were studying sharks off the coast of Rhode Island. Even though I was a little afraid, I joined them.

I thought it would be interesting to get to know these animals better.

We sailed 20 miles (32 km) offshore. The scientists put out some bait. A five-foot (1.5-m)-long blue shark swam up to check it out. I was in the water taking photos. For more than an hour, I drifted in the chilly water. The shark swam right beside me. But it never tried to attack. It just seemed curious. And I was curious about the shark. All my fears melted away. I stared at it in total awe. The shark had a slender body. It had long, winglike fins. It looked like a finely designed aircraft.

Ever since that day, I've been hooked on sharks. I've swum with blue sharks many times since then. I've swum with other kinds, too. Thanks to scientists and explorers, people have begun to better understand sharks. They're no longer seen as monsters. Like lions in the grasslands of Africa, sharks are the top predators in their ocean homes. Predators are animals that hunt other animals for food. But sharks never hunt humans on purpose.

It can be scary to hear about a shark biting a surfer at the beach. But such attacks are very, very rare. A shark may strike if a human threatens it. Or it may mistake a human for a seal or other natural prey. But humans are a greater danger to sharks than they are to us.

Whenever a shark loses a tooth, a new one comes in to replace it. A shark can grow thousands of teeth in its lifetime.

The Scoop on Sharks

Sharks first swam the seas around 400 million years ago. That's almost 200 million years before the first dinosaur walked on Earth. A shark's skeleton is not bony. It's made up mostly of cartilage (sounds like CAR-tuh-lij). Your ears and the tip of your nose are also made of cartilage. Today, there are more than 400 types of shark. The smallest is the dwarf lantern shark. It's smaller than a human hand. The biggest shark is the whale shark (above). It's as long as a school bus!

People kill more than 100 million sharks each year. Most are taken for their fins, which are used in shark fin soup.

Way too often, I see badly hurt sharks. I see some tangled in long fish lines. I see others caught in pieces of plastic trash.

Over the years, I've found it harder and harder to find sharks anywhere. Because of overfishing and pollution, the oceans' great predators are in danger of dying out completely.

Not long ago, I was asked to join a National Geographic expedition (sounds like eks-puh-DISH-un). The members of the expedition were headed to one of the most remote, or faraway, places on the planet. They said I would see a lot of sharks there. So, of course, I jumped at the chance!

A diver explores a reef in the Line Islands. The reddish orange fish are red snappers. They nipped at our fingers and ears!

Chapter 2

FISH BITES!

In the center of the Pacific Ocean is a chain of 11 islands called the Line Islands. Most of the islands belong to the nation of Kiribati (sounds like KEE-ree-bas). Altogether, fewer than 9,000 people live here. On most of the islands, there are no people at all.

Coral reefs ring each of the islands. Reefs are full of nooks and crannies. These make good homes for many kinds of plants and animals. Coral reefs are like the rain forests of the sea. Of all the different types of ocean fish, a third of them make their homes on or near reefs.

Around the Line Islands, reef life has been undisturbed for hundreds of years. That's why National Geographic scientist Enric Sala (sounds like en-REEK SAL-ah) was eager to see the sharks and other wildlife here. He wanted to study an area still untouched by humans.

It was late in March. I flew to Tahiti (sounds like TUH-hee-tee) and met up with Dr. Sala and his crew. We boarded our research ship. It was called the *Hanse Explorer.* We were thrilled to set sail. All around us was the vast, open ocean.

It took us three days to reach the first of the islands we would be studying. It was a tiny island called Flint. My first dive here was awesome. But I knew we were headed for places even more remote.

On the ninth day, we sailed close to Starbuck Island. The water around Starbuck was too shallow for our ship. So we dropped anchor in the deeper water offshore.

We inflated our small rubber boats. Then we lowered them into the water and hopped in. We paddled to a place that looked good for diving. I grabbed my camera and slipped into the water. I knew we were probably the first people to ever dive here.

This reef was like an enchanted forest! I felt caught up in a swirl of color.

I'd explored many coral reefs in the world, but this reef looked thicker. It looked healthier. Deep green algae grew between the corals. Schools of small fish darted over the corals. They nipped at the algae.

I also saw many large predatory fish, such as grouper and red snapper. Out beyond the reef's edge, I saw big tunas. They rocketed past like silver torpedoes.

Most amazing were the sharks. Absolutely everywhere, I saw sharks! I saw blacktip, whitetip, and gray reef sharks. They patrolled the waters, hunting for their next meal. On most reefs today, you're lucky to see even one or two sharks. To find one, you have to set out bait. You have to lure it in. Here, no bait was needed. Here, sharks ruled!

Underwater Flying Saucer

A coral may look like
a plant, or even like a
rock. But it is really a tiny
animal called a polyp (sounds
like PAH-lup). Polyps have soft bodies
with hard outer skeletons. Polyps join
together in groups called colonies. The
colonies can grow for hundreds of years.
A coral reef is a solid structure made of
the skeletons of millions of corals. Near
one of the Line Islands, Kingman Reef, we
discovered a new kind of coral. It had
formed a huge, saucer-shaped colony.
It is more than 500 years old.

I took photographs of the beautiful underwater landscape. It amazed me to think that no humans had ever seen it before.

Dr. Sala and his crew worked hard. They counted fish and tested the water. They checked the health of the coral. Dr. Sala thinks that ten times more sharks live here than on any other reef on the planet.

Some of the sharks seemed curious about me. They moved in close to check me out. Once they had, they just went about their business.

Those red snappers were a different story, though! They had fearsome, needle-sharp teeth. A few looked me over. It seemed like they wanted a taste. Sometimes I had to push them away with my camera. They pestered all of us. They nipped at our ears and fingers. I had the feeling if I were just a little smaller, they would eat me for lunch!

Back on the ship, we had first aid kits loaded with bandages to put on our fish bites and coral scrapes. Places like Starbuck are so remote, you have to bring everything you need with you. We had packed all kinds of safety gear, too. We also had signaling devices, in case we got lost.

We felt proud that we'd planned everything so well. But we were soon to find out that no matter how well you plan, some things you just can't control.

I took this picture of Starbuck Island when I went ashore to explore it with some scientists.

'd been diving in the waters off Starbuck for several days. But I wanted to go ashore to take some photos of the land.

Two of the scientists on the expedition were already on the island. They were studying the seabirds of Starbuck. I decided to join them there. Dr. Sala and my assistant Mauricio Handler came along. National Geographic was making a film of our expedition. A couple of the film crew came, too.

Getting from the ship to the island was a challenge. No boat, not even one of our small rubber boats, could get near the shore. The hard, jagged reef would cut the boat to shreds.

There was only one way to get to Starbuck. We had to swim there! Not only that, I had to put my cameras in a watertight case. Mauricio and I had to tow the case with us as we swam. We struggled to keep from being dashed against the reef by the waves. We were lucky to make it to shore with only a few scrapes and bruises.

Starbuck is very hot and dry. After a few hours of taking photos, we were ready to head back to the ship. But by this time, the sea had changed. Now huge waves were smashing against the shore.

Our captain radioed us. He said it had become too dangerous. There was no way we could swim back to the ship that night. We were stranded! And we had no food, water, or shelter.

The captain had a plan to help us. He kept a rocket gun for just such emergencies. He eased one of the ship's lifeboats as close to the island as he dared. Then he used the gun to shoot a line to shore.

Hope for Sharks

One of the greatest hopes for sharks are marine protected areas. These are sections of the ocean where fishing is strictly limited. So far, less than 2 percent of the ocean is protected. But many people are working hard to make sure more areas will be protected in the future. Dr. Sala continues to work with the local people and the government of Kiribati. They hope to turn the beautiful reefs of the Line Islands into a new marine protected area.

We grabbed the line. On the other end of it, our shipmates attached a waterproof box. It was filled with food, water bottles, and a plastic tarp. We hauled the box through the waves. We hoped it would not smash against the reef and break. Lucky for us, it made it in one piece!

With the tarp and some wood we found on the beach, we built a small shelter. We huddled under it. We were exhausted, hungry, and sunburned. Soon, heavy rain began to pour down. We lay awake most of the night. We wondered what the morning would bring.

As the sun came up, the waves seemed to have calmed down a bit. We decided we would each swim back to the ship with a buddy or two. That way we could help each other if we got into trouble.

But first, we watched the waves. We needed to get an idea of how often the really big ones came in. When we saw a lull, or pause, in the waves, we would swim fast through the shallow water over the dangerous reef. Once we were in the deeper water, we'd be safe.

My swim buddy and I saw a lull in the waves. So she and I began to swim out. Then she hesitated. I turned back to help her. As we tried to make our way through the shallows, I saw a giant wave coming toward us. I shouted for her to put her head down and swim as hard as she could! I took a deep breath and dove under the wave. But not so far under that I would crash against the coral!

We had to dive beneath a couple more of those big waves. Then, finally, we were past the danger zone.

Exhausted and out of breath, we climbed aboard our ship. Everyone made it back safely. As we sailed on to our next stop, we all felt very lucky.

Based on Dr. Sala's studies of the Line Islands, we now have a clearer picture of what a healthy reef looks like. One thing we have learned is that a healthy reef supports lots of sharks and other predatory fish. Understanding the reefs here will help us figure out how to restore reefs that have been polluted and overfished.

I knew that exploring a remote location like Starbuck would be dangerous. But having a chance to take photos in a place few humans ever go is the stuff of dreams. I hope my photos will let people see the beauty of these amazing reefs and get a better understanding of sharks. I hope they'll be inspired to help protect sharks and their wild ocean habitats, all around the world.

THE END

DON'T MISS!

NATIONAL GEOGRAPHIC KiDS **CHAPTERS**

LUCKY LEOPARDS!

And More True Stories of Amazing Animal Rescues

By Aline Alexander Newman

Turn the page for a sneak preview . . .

Runa and Kata
nuzzle each other.
They are as soft
and cuddly as
pet kittens.

Chapter 1

JUNGLE KITTENS

March 2009, Assam, India

People watched their step in the Assam (sounds like ah-SAHM) jungle in northeast India. Roads were few and made of dirt. Trees grew so close together they almost touched. And bushy plants and fallen logs covered the forest floor. You never knew when a hungry tiger or slithering python might surprise you. This place was wild. It belonged to the animals.

Two of those animals lay sleeping in a hollow tree. They were newborn kittens, or cubs. Their mother had left them alone while she went hunting for food. The cubs should have been safe. Except before the mama returned, some woodcutters came.

The woodcutters lived in a village on the edge of the forest, in a part of India called Kokrajhar (sounds like co-kruh-JAR). They earned money by gathering firewood to sell. One man saw the hollow tree. He chopped it down with his ax. The tree landed with a thud. Then he got a big surprise.

Two tiny furballs bounced out! The startled woodcutter dropped his ax. He scooped up the tiny cats. They mewed softly. Their gray spotted coats felt as soft as a baby chick. *What are they?* the man wondered. *Baby tigers or baby leopards?*

It didn't matter. The cubs were adorable. And there was no danger in picking them up. The babies' eyes hadn't even opened yet. *If only I could sell these cats,* he thought.

The woodcutter was very poor. He knew that wild-animal dealers would pay big money for the cubs. Then the dealers would sell the cubs for even more money. Rich collectors from other countries paid thousands of dollars for wild animals to put in their backyard zoos.

Even if no dealers came along, the cubs were a good find. Maybe the woodcutter could sell them as pets. Or his neighbors might buy them. Some men tied animal parts to their swords. This was a custom, or tradition, in his village. Some people hung animal skins up to decorate their huts. Local healers also used animal parts to make medicine.

The woodcutter knew it was wrong to capture wild animals. It was wrong to sell them too. The Indian government had laws against these things. But the thought of all the money he could make dazzled him. What if he could make $200 selling the cubs? That would be like winning the lottery! With that much money he could feed his family for many months.

The woodcutter carried the cubs home. Then he quietly spread the word. He had jungle cats for sale.

But his plan went wrong. He didn't know how to take care of the cubs. He didn't know how to feed them. Or even what to feed them! Another villager became worried. He told a forest department worker named Akhim (sounds like ah-KEEM) about the cubs. Akhim went to the woodcutter. He demanded the kittens. The woodcutter turned them over.

Akhim rushed the baby cats to the local wildlife rescue center. It was run by the Wildlife Trust of India. It was not a moment too soon. The cubs hadn't eaten in days. "One of them was seriously sick," says Sonali Ghosh (sounds like so-NAH-lee GOUSH). Sonali is an officer with the Indian Forest Service. "I was scared it might die," she said.

The rescue center veterinarians (sounds like vet-er-ih-NARE-ee-ens) examined the baby cats. "These are common leopards," the vets decided. The common leopard is the kind most "commonly" seen. There are also snow leopards, clouded leopards, and Sunda clouded leopards.

Everyone at the rescue center treated the cubs with great care. Workers fed the kittens around the clock. They gave them goat's milk, using baby bottles.

Leopards are meat-eaters. So the vets wanted the cubs to get a taste for meat. After about three weeks, the workers started mixing liver soup in with the goat's milk.

The cubs ate a lot. They grew fast. As they got bigger, the markings on their coats became easier to see. One day the vets noticed something very interesting. The spots on these cubs looked different from the spots on common leopards. They were darker and grayer.

The vets looked at each other. They wondered . . .

Could it be?

Yes! These cubs weren't common leopards after all. They were clouded leopards. Extremely rare, almost never seen, clouded leopards!

INDEX

MORE INFORMATION

To find more information about the animal species featured in this book, check out these books and websites.

National Geographic Kids Everything Sharks, by Ruth A. Musgrave, National Geographic, 2011

Ocean Soul, by Brian Skerry, National Geographic, 2011

A Whale on Her Own, by Brian Skerry, Blackbirch Press, 2000

National Geographic "Animals: Coral"
animals.nationalgeographic.com/animals/
invertebrates/coral

National Geographic "Animals: Sharks"
animals.nationalgeographic.com/animals/sharks

National Geographic Kids "Creature Features: Belugas"
kids.nationalgeographic.com/kids/animals/
creaturefeature/belugas

National Geographic Kids "Creature Features: Harp Seals"
kids.nationalgeographic.com/kids/animals/
creaturefeature/harp-seals

National Geographic Kids "Creature Features:
Leatherback Sea Turtles"
kids.nationalgeographic.com/kids/animals/creaturefeature/
leatherback-sea-turtle

For Katherine and Caroline—B. S.
For Geoffrey—K. W. Z.

CREDITS

Cover and all interior photos are by Brian Skerry unless noted here:
19, William West/AFP/Getty Images; 72, Flip Nicklin/Minden
Pictures; 101, © IFAW/WTI S. Kadur; 102, © IFAW/WTI A. Mookerjee

ACKNOWLEDGMENTS

I am most grateful to *National Geographic* magazine for commissioning me to produce photographs and stories. I especially wish to thank Editor in Chief Chris Johns, Director of Photography Sarah Leen, Deputy Director of Photography Ken Geiger, and Senior Editor for Natural History Kathy Moran for their support of my work.

So much of my work relies on the expertise of dedicated professionals from many disciplines in locations worldwide. Assisting me with the projects written about in this book are the following people, to whom I give great thanks: Scott Benson, Barbara Block, Mario Cyr, Scott Eckert, Mike Hammill, Mauricio Handler, Mike James, Jim Johnson, Rod Mast, Tom Mulloy, Enric Sala, Becky Sjare, Kelly Stewart, Sean Whelan, and Jeff Wildermuth.

Finally, I wish to thank my wife, Marcia, and daughters, Kate and Caroline, for their loving support and inspiration. — *Brian Skerry*